D0907692

The Alphabet

Say the name of each letter of the alphabet.

The Letter A

A

✏️ Help the angel find her halo.
Follow the path of pictures that begin with **A**.

✏️ Trace and write the letters.

Jolly ABCs & 123s

© School Zone Publishing Company 02681

Color the picture.

1 = tan   2 = yellow   3 = light blue   4 = green   5 = blue

 Trace and write the letters.

Jolly ABCs & 123s

B

 Look at the pictures.
Circle the pictures that start with **B**.

 Trace and write the letters.

b

Help Santa get the boat to the reindeer.
Follow the path of **b**'s.

START

b b b

b

b b

b

b p

b b

b

a

END

b b

d

Trace and write the letters.

5

Jolly ABCs & 123s

C

Crystal Castle has things in it that begin with **C**. Write the letter **C** under the pictures that begin with **C**.

Trace and write the letters.

Calvin is looking for the other Christmas carolers.
Follow the path of pictures that begin with **c** to
help Calvin find the carolers.

START

END

Trace and write the letters.

Jolly ABCs & 123s

D

✏️ Help Dee follow the path of pictures that begin with **D** to the dollhouse.

START

END

✏️ Trace and write the letters.

D D

The Letter d

Drew Dinosaur is looking for things that begin with **d**. Write the letter **d** under the pictures that begin with **d** to see what Drew found.

Trace and write the letters.

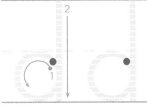

Jolly ABCs & 123s

E

 Elmer Elf is looking for the letter **E**.
Circle the gifts with the letter **E** on them.

 How many did you find? _____

 Trace and write the letters.

Jolly ABCs & 123s   © School Zone Publishing Company 02681

The elephant likes to get peanuts as a gift.
Color the peanuts that have the letter **e** on them.

How many did you find? _____

Trace and write the letters.

Jolly ABCs & 123s

The Letter F

F

✏️ The foxes like to hide among the fir trees.
Find and circle **6** foxes.

 Trace and write the letters.

The fox collects festive flags.
Circle **4** flags that have pictures that begin with **f**.

Trace and write the letters.

Jolly ABCs & 123s

The Letter G

🖊 Circle the things in the gingerbread house that begin with **G**.

🖊 Write the letter **G** under the pictures you circled.

🖊 Trace and write the letters.

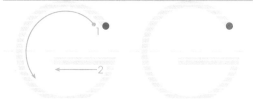

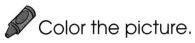

🖍️ Color the picture.

1 = brown   2 = light blue   3 = blue   4 = red   5 = green

✏️ Trace and write the letters.

g g

a b c d e f g h i j k l m n o p q r s t u v w x y z

15

H

Find the things in the house that begin with **H**.
Write the letter **H** under the pictures that begin with **H**.

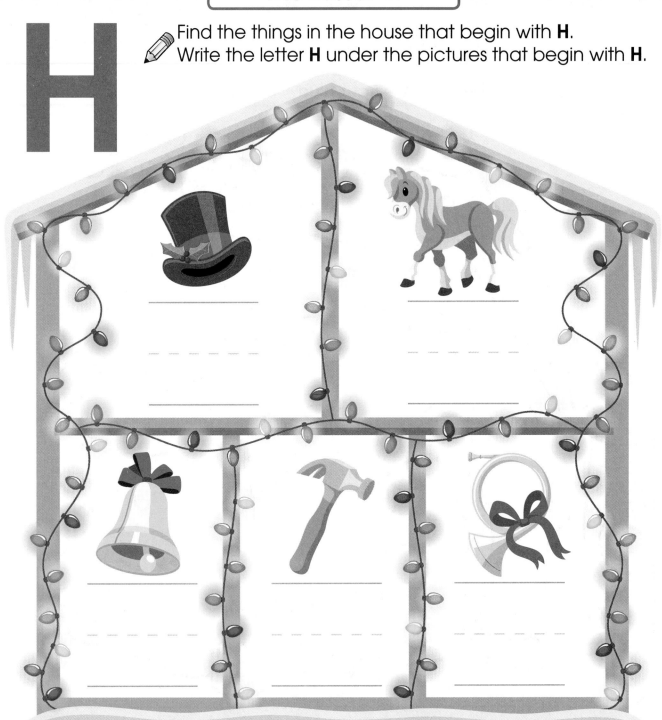

Trace and write the letters.

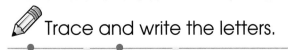

A B C D E F G H I J K L M N O P Q R S T U V W X Y Z

Jolly ABCs & 123s

h

🖍 Say the name of each picture.
🖍 Color the pictures that begin with **h**.

✏️ Trace and write the letters.

Jolly ABCs & 123s

I Write the letter **I** under the pictures that begin with **I**.

 Trace and write the letters.

Jolly ABCs & 123s

i

The iguana has lost her way in the north pole.
Follow the path of **i**'s to help Izzy get to Santa's workshop.

END

g s i i i i

j z i o i h i

i i i j i i i

i j n c a f j

START i u j t c n v

Trace and write the letters.

2

1

Jolly ABCs & 123s

The Letter J

Jack Frost is jogging through the snow to get to the pictures that begin with **J**.

 Draw a line to show where Jack will go.

J

START

END

 Trace and write the letters.

J J

The Letter j

j

How many gifts can the juggler keep in the air?
Circle **4** gifts that have pictures that begin with **j**.

Trace and write the letters.

j

Jolly ABCs & 123s

The Letter K

Help Kris Kringle find his kitten.
Follow the path of pictures that begin with **K**.

START

END

Trace and write the letters.

The Letter k

k

Help Santa find the pictures that begin with **k**.
Say the name of each picture.
Color the pictures that begin with **k**.

🖊 Trace and write the letters.

k k

a b c d e f g h i j k l m n o p q r s t u v w x y z

Jolly ABCs & 123s

Help the lion find things that begin with **L**.
Color the lights that have pictures that begin with **L**.

 How many did you find? _____

Trace and write the letters.

Which Santa sweaters will be washed today?
Write the letter I under the sweaters that have pictures that begin with I. Then draw lines from those shirts to the washer.

 Trace and write the letters.

Jolly ABCs & 123s

The Letter M

Help Mr. Claus find his other mitten.
Follow the trail of pictures that begin with **M**.

START

END

 Trace and write the letters.

M M M M

Jolly ABCs & 123s

m

Help the snow monster find things that begin with **m**. Draw lines from the pictures that begin with **m** to the snow monster.

Trace and write the letters.

Jolly ABCs & 123s

N

🖉 Help Ned find his way to the north pole.
Follow the trail of nickels.

🖉 Trace and write the letters.

The nutcracker is looking for things that begin with **n**.
Help him by circling the pictures that begin with **n**.

| necklace | nest | nut | net |

Trace and write the letters.

The Letter O

Help the owl get to the box of ornaments.
Draw a path to get to the ornaments.

START

END

Trace and write the letters.

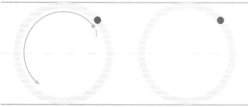

A B C D E F G H I J K L M N O P Q R S T U V W X Y Z

The Letter o

Ollie Octopus wants to know which things begin with **o**.
Write the letter **o** under the pictures that begin with **o**.

Trace and write the letters.

Jolly ABCs & 123s

P

Polly Penguin is in a parade.
Circle all the pictures that begin with **P**.

 Trace and write the letters.

P P

Jolly ABCs & 123s

© School Zone Publishing Company 02681

The Letter p

Help the polar bear get to his party.
Follow the path of pictures that begin with **p**.

Trace and write the letters.

 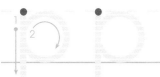

Jolly ABCs & 123s

The Letter Q

Queen Quinn is making a quilt.
Color all of the **Q**'s you can find.

How many did you find? _____

Trace and write the letters.

The Letter q

Help the queen bring presents to the quails.
Follow the path of **q**'s.

START q q q q q q q

a	p	d	a	p	d	q
q	q	q	q	q	q	q
q	p	a	p	d	a	p
q	q	q	q	p	p	p

END

Trace and write the letters.

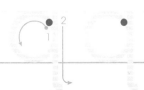

Jolly ABCs & 123s

The Letter R

R

✏️ Help Rachel Rabbit put away things that begin with **R**.
✏️ Draw lines to show where the things go.

✏️ Trace and write the letters.

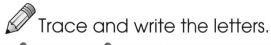

r

Help the reindeer find all of the words that begin with **r**.
Write the letter **r** under the pictures that begin with **r**.

Trace and write the letters.

Jolly ABCs & 123s

The Letter S

Santa's workshop is full of animals!
Write the letter **S** under the animals that begin with **S**.

Trace and write the letters.

Help the seal match the pictures that begin with **s**.
Draw a line between each pair of pictures that go together.

 Trace and write the letters.

Jolly ABCs & 123s

T

Tammy Tinsel is looking for things that begin with **T**. Help her by circling the pictures that begin with **T**.

Trace and write the letters.

A B C D E F G H I J K L M **40** N O P Q R S T U V W X Y Z

The Letter t

Tommy and Tina are in a toboggan race.
The winner is the one that finds the most pictures that begin with **t**.

 Circle the pictures that begin with **t**.

 Then circle the winner of the race.

 Trace and write the letters.

Jolly ABCs & 123s

U

Help Ulmer unwrap the gifts by circling the boxes that have the letter **U** on them.

Trace and write the letters.

Uma is looking at all the gifts.
Circle the pictures that begin with the letter **u**.

Trace and write the letters.

a b c d e f g h i j k l m n o p q r s t u v w x y z

Jolly ABCs & 123s

V

✏️ Vicky is looking for things that begin with **V**.
✏️ Find and circle the pictures that begin with **V**.

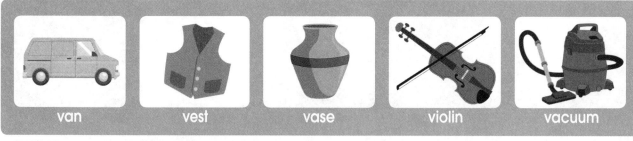

| van | vest | vase | violin | vacuum |

✏️ Trace and write the letters.

Help Vivian find all of the ornaments with **v** on them.
Color the ornaments that have the letter **v** on them.

Trace and write the letters.

Jolly ABCs & 123s

W

Wally wants to put things that begin with **W** on his holiday wreath.
Draw lines from the pictures that begin with **W** to Wally's wreath.

 Trace and write the letters.

W W W

The winter wren wants to get to the well.
Follow the path of pictures that begin with **w**.

W

START

END

Trace and write the letters.

1 2 3 4 W W

Jolly ABCs & 123s

The Letter X

 Circle all the **X**'s you can find in the picture.

X

 Trace and write the letters.

X X X

Jolly ABCs & 123s   © School Zone Publishing Company 02681

The Letter x

X

✏️ Follow the path of **x**'s to get Santa to the rooftop.

START

v	s	x	v	x	x	x	x
x	x	x	y	x	y	y	x
x	w	v	h	x	l	l	x
x	x	x	x	x	v	x	u
q	u	w	j	n	s	x	r

END

✏️ Trace and write the letters.

Jolly ABCs & 123s

Y

Help Yolanda find all of the yellow yo-yos.
Color the yo-yos that have the letter **Y** on them *yellow*.

Yellow
yo-yos

 Trace and write the letters.

© School Zone Publishing Company 02681

✏️ Draw a line through the letter **y** and the pictures that begin with **y**.

y

✏️ Trace and write the letters.

Jolly ABCs & 123s

Z

 Help Zippy Zebra find his way through the maze.
Follow the path of **Z**'s to help Zippy get to Santa.

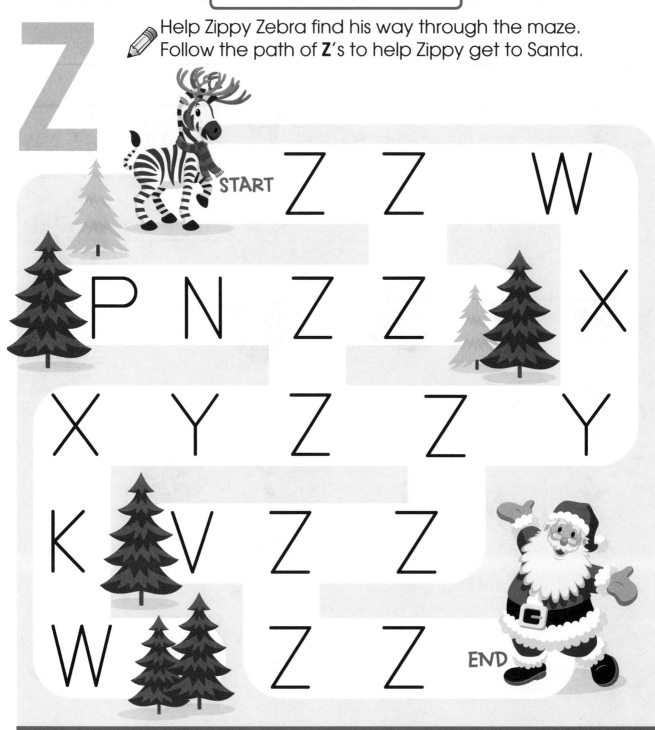

START

Z Z W

P N Z Z X

X Y Z Z Y

K V Z Z

W Z Z END

 Trace and write the letters.

Z

The Letter z

Help Zippy Zebra find his zebra friends.
Circle all the zebras you can find in the picture.

Z

Trace and write the letters.

a b c d e f g h i j k l m n o p q r s t u v w x y z

© School Zone Publishing Company 02681

Jolly ABCs & 123s

0
zero

This basket has **0** 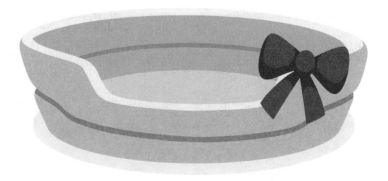 in it.

 Trace and write the number **0**.

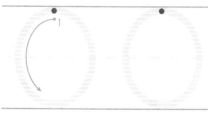

 Circle the puppies with **0** bows on them.

Circle the trees that have **0** ornaments on them.

 Trace and write **zero**.

Jolly ABCs & 123s

1

Count 1 .

one

.

 Trace and write the number 1.

 Circle the groups of 1.

Color I  red.

Color I 🧸 brown.

✏️ Trace and write **one**.

Jolly ABCs & 123s

2
two
• •

Count 2

 Trace and write the number **2**.

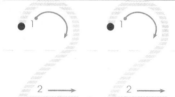

 Circle the groups of **2**.

Color the **1**'s **red**.

 Color the **2**'s **black**.

 Trace and write **two**.

Jolly ABCs & 123s

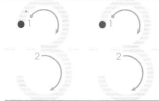

Count 3 .

 Trace and write the number **3**.

Circle the groups of **3**.

 How many can you find?

 Trace and write **three**.

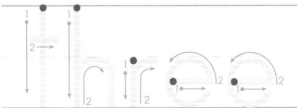

　　　　　　　Jolly ABCs & 123s

Count **4**

four
●●●●

 Trace and write the number **4**.

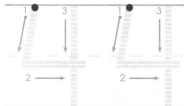

 Circle the groups of **4**.

Color the ⬭ **yellow**.

 Color the 👗 **blue**.

 Trace and write **four**.

Jolly ABCs & 123s

5
five
• • • • •

Count 5 .

 Trace and write the number **5**.

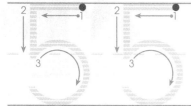

 Circle the groups of **5**.

Jolly ABCs & 123s

© School Zone Publishing Company 02681

Circle the ornaments with **5** stars on it.

 Trace and write **five**.

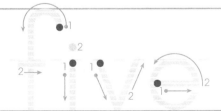

Jolly ABCs & 123s

Count **6** .

6
six
• • • • •
•

 Trace and write the number **6**.

6 6

 Circle the groups of **6**.

Jolly ABCs & 123s

© School Zone Publishing Company 02681

Trace  to make a group of **6** snowflakes.

 Trace and write **six**.

Jolly ABCs & 123s

7
seven
●●●●
●●

Count **7** .

✏️ Trace and write the number **7**.

✏️ Circle the groups of **7**.

Draw a line through the **7**'s to get to the finish.

START

6 4 7 7 7 5 1 7 7 7 7 3 4 7 3 2 1 2 7 1 5 END

 Trace and write **seven**.

Jolly ABCs & 123s

8
eight

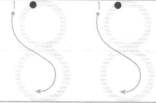

Count **8** .

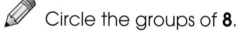 Trace and write the number **8**.

 Circle the groups of **8**.

Each  has one that looks just like it.

✏️ Draw a line between each pair of matching cookies.

✏️ Trace and write **eight**.

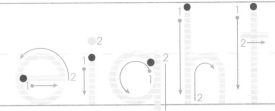

© School Zone Publishing Company 02681

Jolly ABCs & 123s

9
nine

Count 9

 Trace and write the number 9.

 Circle the groups of 9.

Color **9** green.

 Circle **9** birds.

 Trace and write **nine**.

10
ten

Count 10

 Trace and write the number **10**.

 Circle the groups of **10**.

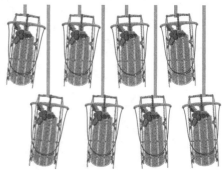

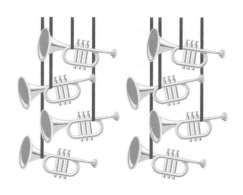

Color **10** ⭕ **red**.

Circle **10** 🍬.

Trace and write **ten**.

11
eleven

Count 11

 Trace and write the number 11.

 Circle the groups of 11.

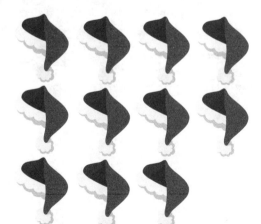

 Circle **11**.

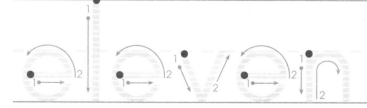 Trace and write **eleven**.

eleven

12
twelve

Count 12 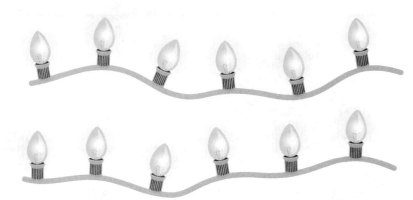.

 Trace and write the number **12**.

 Circle the groups of **12**.

0 1 2 3 4 5 6 7 8 9 10 11 12 13 14 15 16 17 18 19 20

78

How many can you find?

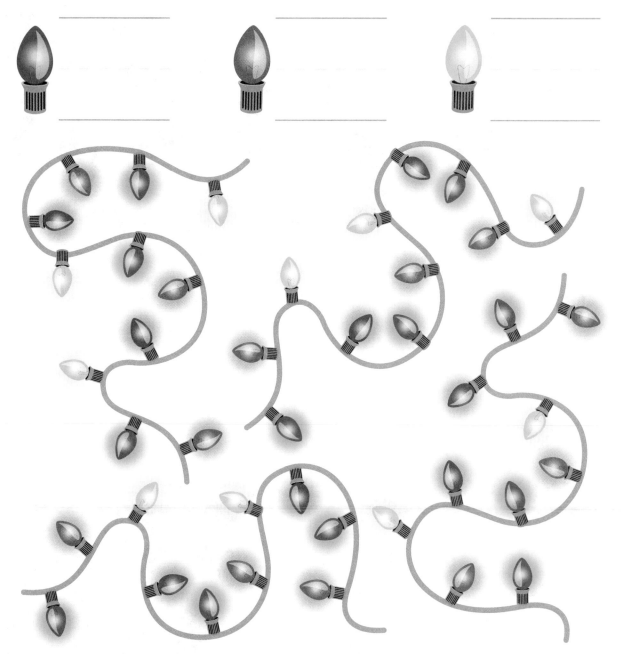

_____   _____   _____

 Trace and write **twelve**.

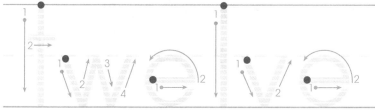

Jolly ABCs & 123s

13
thirteen

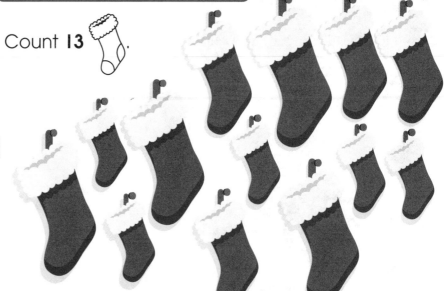

Count 13 🧦.

 Trace and write the number **13**.

 Circle the group of **13**.

Draw more to make a group of **13**.

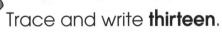 Trace and write **thirteen**.

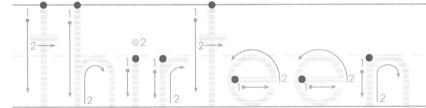

Jolly ABCs & 123s

14
fourteen

Count 14 ☃.

 Trace and write the number **14**.

 Circle the groups of **14**.

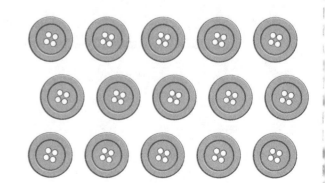

Jolly ABCs & 123s

Color **14** red.

Check **14** .

How many ?

Trace and write **fourteen**.

fourteen

© School Zone Publishing Company 02681

Jolly ABCs & 123s

15
fifteen

Count 15 .

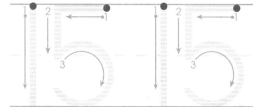

 Trace and write the number 15.

 Circle the groups of 15.

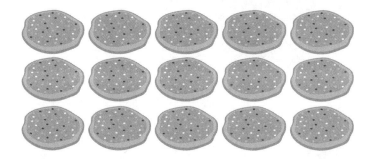

Draw a line through the **15**'s to get the gifts to the snowman.

START

15   15
15   15
15
15   15
5   15
15   13
11   15   15   15
15
10   15
7   15
8
14   15
12   4   9   15   15   END

 Trace and write **fifteen**.

Jolly ABCs & 123s

16
sixteen

Count 16 .

 Trace and write the number 16.

16 16

 Circle the groups of 16.

Each  has one that looks just like it.

✏️ Draw a line between each pair of matching mittens.

✏️ Trace and write **sixteen**.

sixteen

Count **17** .

17
seventeen

 Trace and write the number **17**.

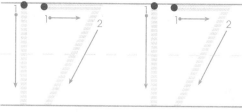

Circle the groups of **17**.

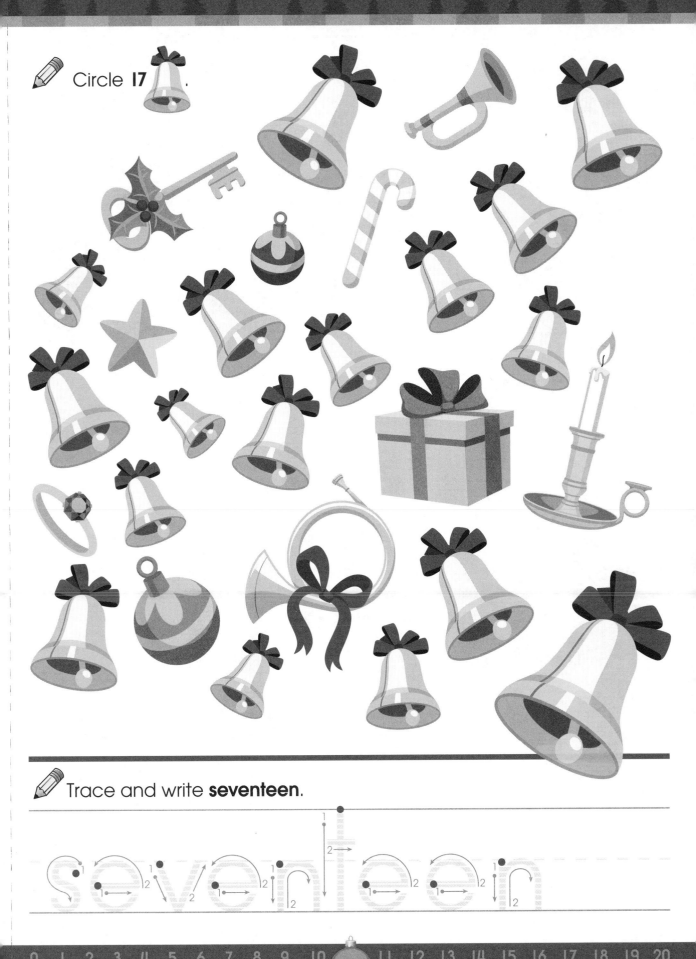

Circle **17** .

Trace and write **seventeen**.

seventeen

Jolly ABCs & 123s

18
eighteen

Count 18 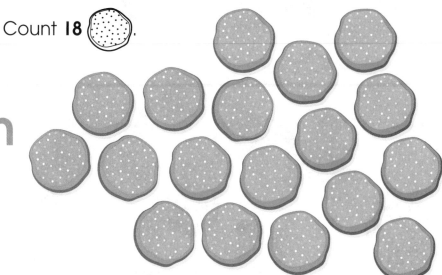.

 Trace and write the number **18**.

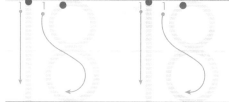

 Circle the group of **18**.

How many can you find?

 _____   _____   _____

_____   _____   _____

 Trace and write **eighteen**.

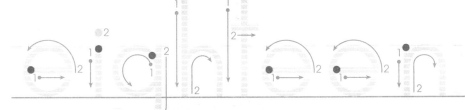

Jolly ABCs & 123s

19
nineteen

Count 19 .

 Trace and write the number 19.

19 19

 Circle the group of 19.

Color **19** purple.

Check **19** ●.

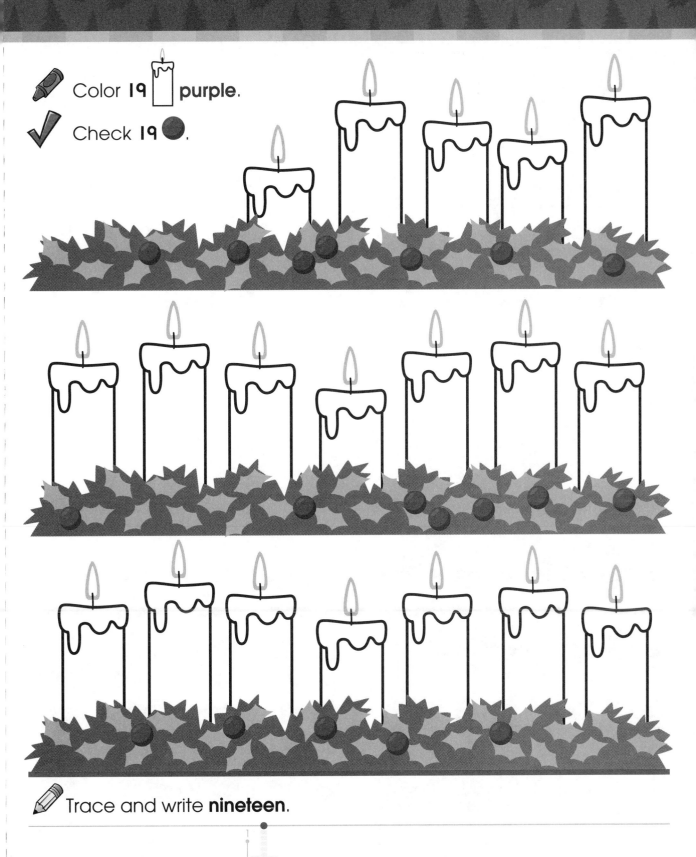

✏️ Trace and write **nineteen**.

nineteen

Jolly ABCs & 123s

20
twenty

Count 20 .

 Trace and write the number **20**.

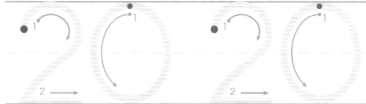

 Circle the group of **20**.

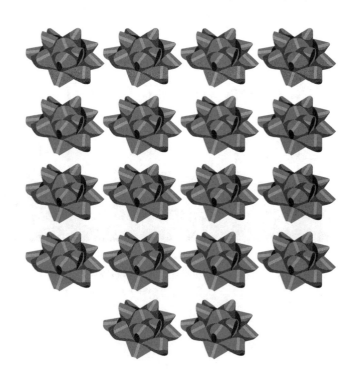

Trace the path from **1** to **20**.

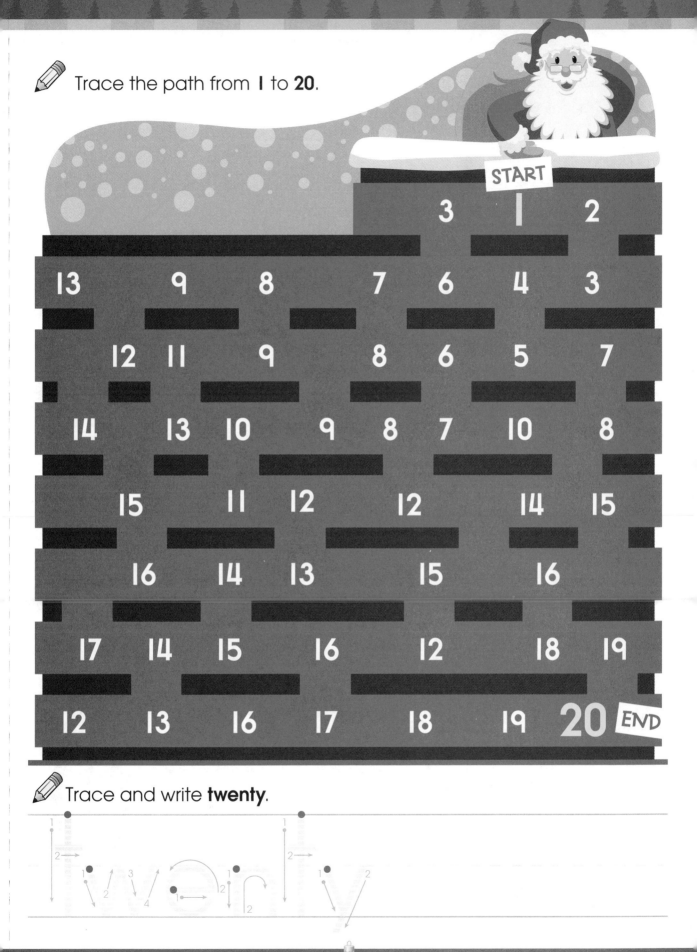

Trace and write **twenty**.

Jolly ABCs & 123s

Connect the dots from **1** to **20**.
Color the picture.

Jolly ABCs & 123s 02681